A PAIR OF POLAR BEARS

Twin Cubs Find a Home at the San Diego Zoo

by Joanne Ryder

photos by the World-Famous San Diego Zoo

Simon & Schuster Books
for Young Readers
New York   London   Toronto   Sydney

To Matthew and Sam Yep, two GREAT great-nephews, with love—J. R.

Acknowledgments

The author is especially grateful to the Research, Animal Care, and Marketing staffs at the World-Famous San Diego Zoo for their insight, graciousness, and care in the preparation and review of this manuscript, and thanks them for their kind and thoughtful assistance. Also, I thank my editors, Alexandra Cooper and David Gale, for their understanding, skill, and guidance in helping an author tell her tale of two endearing bears.

SIMON & SCHUSTER BOOKS FOR YOUNG READERS

An imprint of Simon & Schuster Children's Publishing Division

1230 Avenue of the Americas, New York, New York 10020

Text copyright © 2006 by Joanne Ryder

Photographs copyright © 2001, 2002, 2003 by the Zoological Society of San Diego

Photograph compilation copyright © 2006 by the Zoological Society of San Diego

All rights reserved, including the right of reproduction in whole or in part in any form.

SIMON & SCHUSTER BOOKS FOR YOUNG READERS is a trademark of Simon & Schuster, Inc.

Book design by Lucy Ruth Cummins

The text for this book is set in Egyptienne.

Manufactured in China

2 4 6 8 10 9 7 5 3 1

Library of Congress Cataloging-in-Publication Data

Ryder, Joanne. · A pair of polar bears : twin cubs find a home at the San Diego Zoo / Joanne Ryder.— 1st ed.

p. cm. · ISBN-13: 978-0-689-85871-0 · ISBN-10: 0-689-85871-X

1. Polar bear—Infancy—California—San Diego—Juvenile literature. 2. San Diego Zoo—Juvenile literature. I. Title.

QL737.C27R93 2006 · 599.786—dc22 2005014013

At the top of the world
two little polar bears
are found,
all alone and helpless.
A brother and sister
make the biggest journey
of their short lives
to a new home
far, far away.

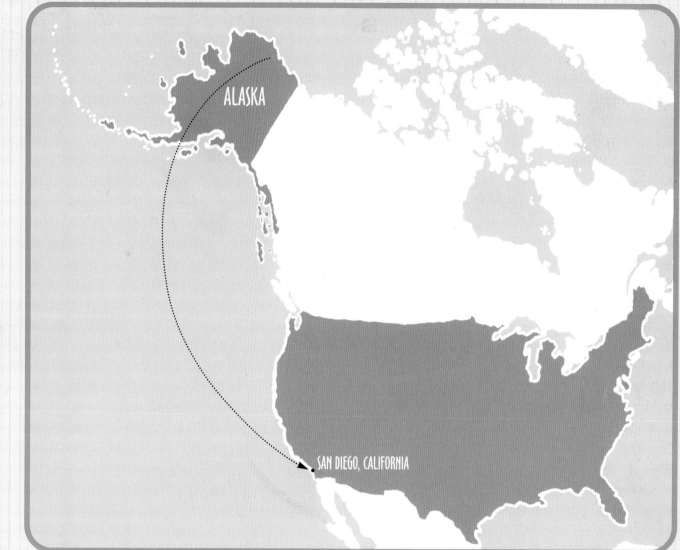

ALASKA

SAN DIEGO, CALIFORNIA

When orphan polar bear twins were rescued in northern Alaska, wildlife biologists knew the cubs were in trouble. Only three months old, the cubs no longer had a mother to protect them, feed them, and teach them how to hunt for food. The twins needed a new home . . . soon.

The World-Famous San Diego Zoo offered them a home in its Polar Bear Plunge exhibit. The small male and female cubs were safely flown thousands of miles from their snowy world to a new life in southern California.

Tiny travelers arrive in a safe place where new friends welcome them and watch over them.

Before the cubs could settle into the Polar Bear Plunge habitat, they had to stay thirty days in quarantine in the zoo hospital. The San Diego Zoo Keepers fed and took good care of the twins.

The keepers prepared a special rich formula to help the cubs grow. And grow they did! The cubs were small for their age, weighing just twelve and seventeen pounds when they came to the zoo. But soon they began gaining weight—an average of fourteen pounds a week!

A hungry cub
laps and laps
a tasty meal
and licks herself clean.

Nose to nose,
twins sniff
and touch
each other's furry face,
familiar and friendly,
in a different place.

 The twins share a strong bond. Sometimes a loud sound or strange object scared one or both. Then they quickly ran to find each other. Polar bear twins in the wild would behave just the same way. A reassuring touch helped each feel safe, and the cubs were confident to explore again.

Climbing
and chasing,
carefree cubs
make up
their own
bear games.
It's good
to rest together
in a cozy spot.

The little cubs slept in small puppy crates and enjoyed climbing on them too. The keepers added other objects for the cubs to encounter. They wanted the cubs to feel comfortable with logs, balls, dirt, and hay—things they would later find in the polar bear exhibit. The twins were interested in everything. They even liked to eat the dirt!

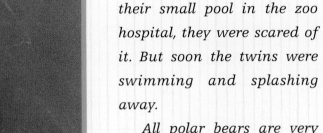

When the twins first saw their small pool in the zoo hospital, they were scared of it. But soon the twins were swimming and splashing away.

All polar bears are very fine swimmers. In the wild, many roam the ice-covered seas all winter long, hunting for seals. Their Latin name, Ursus maritimus, *means Sea Bear.*

Cautious
but curious,
the cubs
pause, sniff . . .
then take a chance!
Two brave, wet bears
discover how much fun
swimming can be.

The cubs finally made their big move to the Polar Bear Plunge exhibit. They had big "bedrooms" now where they were fed. Here, Senior Animal Trainer JoAnne Simerson feeds a cub using a syringe. The cubs learned to separate when eating. Otherwise the bigger male cub would have taken his sister's share too. He loved to eat!

Look at
Kalluk
the athlete!
He loves
playing ball,
tossing things,
and making
lots of noise.

After much thought and care, the zoo named the twins. The names reflect the twins' Alaskan homeland and the native Inuit people living there.

The large polar bear exhibit was made to resemble the arctic land in summer. The bears could climb hills and logs, dig in the dirt, or sunbathe on the flat rocks.

Young explorers
play follow
the leader
and
learn about
a new place—
step by step
and
scent by scent.

The bears were introduced to their new habitat a bit at a time—first, their bedrooms, then a small area outside. Of all the new things they saw, the blue sky overhead seemed the most amazing.

Moving outside,
white bears
look up,
gazing at
the sky—
so big, so blue.

Tatqiq
has a face
round and bright
like the full moon.
She is
precise,
graceful,
and
a thinker.

The male cub is Kalluk (Ka-look), the Inuit word meaning thunder. His sister is Tatqiq (Tot-keek), which means moon.

While Kalluk
belly flops,
Tatqiq
takes her time
and
points her toes,
diving with
bear style.

 *The bears' new home had a stream and a huge pool—the Plunge. The water was chilled, unlike the small pool at the zoo hospital. The cold water surprised the cubs at first. But soon they loved a cool dip after playing or sunbathing.*

After a swim,
lively cubs
roll and roll,
changing from
white bears
to brown bears.

 The twins liked to roll in the dirt. They used the dirt to dry off after a swim. Their fur got dry, but dirty. When clean, a polar bear's fur looks white. But it really isn't. Each hair is a clear hollow tube. Sunlight, bouncing off a bear's fur, makes it look white.

Large windows in the exhibit allow visitors to view the bears—and the curious bears watch the visitors, too. The two-inch acrylic glass let cubs and visitors meet safely.

Broad paws touch
the smooth glass
as small eager hands
reach toward them.

Clever bears
turn small gifts
and surprises
into tools
and toys.

The zoo set up a special program for the twins. The goal was to let the cubs think on their own and entertain themselves. The bears enjoyed finding unfamiliar objects—balls, large bones, sacks, barrels, palm leaves, seaweed, and snow—and seeing what they could do with each.

Furry cubs
celebrate
their own
snow day,
tasting snow,
enjoying
its coldness,
and sliding
down
on slippery
tummies.

The twins enjoyed a winter treat. The zoo made a snowy playground just for them. They played the games every polar bear naturally knows.

Polar bears are very intelligent animals. They use objects as tools to get something done. One day the cubs wanted a toy that was out of reach. They looked around and saw a large block of plastic ice. They pushed the block to just the right spot. Then the cubs climbed on top and recovered their toy.

Still playful friends,
a sister and brother
have grown
in size and wisdom,
sharing discoveries
and adventures
in their new life.

Tatqiq and Kalluk have made a long journey from the top of the world. They are no longer tiny and helpless. Today the twins are intelligent and capable bears. These engaging cubs remind us of all the polar bears in the wild. They help us remember that all bears need a safe, clean, and good home too.